THE HEALING JOURNAL

A Journey to Self-Discovery & Healing on Purpose

M. S. RICE

The Healing Journal

© 2018 by M. S. Rice

ISBN 978-0-578-45216-6

Suicide Hotline –https://suicidepreventionlifeline.org

Quote by F. Scott Fitzgerald

"Faith without work is dead." **KJV 2:14-26, verse 20**

Edited by Patricia Rice, MBA.

I dedicate this book to B. Smith-Flowers, SIP, a fellow dreamer and creative beauty, Mommy. I love and miss you dearly.

To the rest of my family and friends, thank you for all your love, support and belief in me. Without all your support, I wouldn't have been able to complete this journey.

TABLE OF CONTENTS

There is nothing you can't recover from, if you invest in the time to heal from it.

-M. S. Rice

MY STARTING OVER JOURNEY

Hello and welcome! I wanted to explain as briefly as I could the reason why I wrote this book. The creation of this journal has been many years in the making, however, the summer of 2018, really brought the concept for this book into focus.

What started out as a summer with so many great possibilities, it kind of ended up being a nightmare. I went through so many ups and downs that I literally felt like I was being attacked. Throw in a little near-death experience and life really got interesting. In July 2018, I was admitted to the hospital because I had developed extensive blood clots in both of my lungs. It's a dangerous situation when you have one or two blood clots in the lungs but in the words of one of my nurses, "I had a crap load!" As a person who rarely gets a head cold, you can imagine, what a scary ordeal it was to hear such a serious diagnosis. It didn't make sense to develop so many clots, all at once, and yet there I was. I have been thankful every day since, knowing that I still had some time left on the clock.

As cliché as it sounds, living through a near-death experience is one way to have you rethinking your life and the direction it's going. I had to perform hard assessments of my life, both past and present, to see if I would have been happy with the legacy that I would've left behind. The truth was, I wasn't unhappy with my life, so much as I was feeling unfulfilled in it. It was never clearer to me that life really was too short to have *any* regrets left on the table. Time really isn't on anyone's side. Right now, is all we really have, and we will never know the day nor the hour, when our time is up. What a sobering thought that was. Especially since, I still had things that I wanted to do and experience in this life. If July 2018 would have been it, it would have simply been left undone.

Four years ago, back in 2014, I started my journey to self-discovery and healing on purpose. I set out on a quest to figure out exactly who I was and why I always seem to end up at some sort of crossroads every few years. I had just been through a major breakup, so mentally and emotionally, I was in shambles. I wasn't in the best mental space to take care of myself, yet I was handling things the best that I could. I was still going to work every day. I wasn't going without the things that I truly needed. I was making it day by day. I was "adulting" for sure, but the only problem was that I was hating every minute of it. I woke-up in tears, I cried throughout the day, only to come home and eventually cried myself to sleep. I felt stuck in this never-ending loop of my despair. All the ugly parts of depression were rearing its ugly head, all at once, and for the first time I was too powerless to stop it. I willingly fell down the rabbit hole, with no way out. Like many of us who must fight through depression every single day, every day wasn't a bad day, they just weren't great days either. I felt, as if, I was at constant war with myself. I wanted to feel better and do better but was constantly nursing my pain.

One day I woke up and I had, had enough. Enough of the crying. Enough of replaying bad memories. Enough of thinking it was no use in trying to feel better. Since, bad things were just lurking around every corner. I decided that I couldn't waste another day mourning all my pain, my disappointments and my regrets. I had to get control over my emotions and my mind and take charge of my life again. I found myself wanting to get better and to get over my past and present pain for good. I made the decision that I wanted to go back to counseling, but I felt I needed a plan. I didn't want to go to counseling and end up drawing blanks in the middle of a session, not knowing where to start. I wanted to be able to get to the good stuff right off the bat. I started pouring over my journals and picking out whatever memory still held pain for me or whatever I needed a different perspective on. I didn't just jot down a painful event, I fully expressed in writing why it still bothered me in detail. I didn't care how far I had to go back to my get the unpleasant memories. I figured, if I still remembered them, they still must be valid.

And, boy! Talk about getting things out of your system. The more I wrote the better I felt. I was able to look at some issues differently, without anyone's help. I was starting to feel better, very early on in the process, just by getting things out of my head and on to paper. That act alone provided me with such tremendous relief. So much so, that for years I thought that I had healed and that my journey was over. Even though I still felt lost at times, for the most part, my life was good. It would take a few more years to realize my mistake. I had no follow-up plan. I just tackled the pain and left the future a complete unknown. Huge mistake!

Fast forward back to July 2018, three days after I was discharged out of the hospital, I sat down and wrote the outline for this book. It was during that time, that it occurred to me that my journey was still unfinished. I still had work to do. For years I was just coasting along in life but not feeling as if I was truly living, but just existing. So, when the book outline started to take shape, I knew that planning for your future had to be included for the whole journey to make sense. It would have been nice to figure all of this out a lot sooner, but it's better late than never.

I created this journal for the people who need help in moving forward that may feel their past or present is holding them back. All the while, taking the guess-work out of figuring out what to do next, after you heal. Now I will not downplay this process at all, things will get emotionally and mentally draining, but going back is truly the only way to move forward. This journal is not a what to do in order to feel better. I focused my efforts on creating something that would help a person get everything all out. That way, you can decide if you would like to pursue counseling as a next step. What better way to get started with counseling, knowing exactly what needs to be addressed? I am not a licensed therapist. But I do encourage the use of one. Deciding to heal on purpose is the best thing that you can do for yourself. You will never be able to live a positive life, if you are constantly dwelling in negativity. *Life is too short to keep enduring a life where you can't find peace in your past, joy in your present and hope for your future.* You must reprioritize the things that matter to you, in your life and start shaking things up.

I have always felt that one of my callings or purpose in life was to help people, in some capacity. Since giving people unsolicited advice that they haven't asked for is something that I excel at, I figured why not write this book! ☺   I appreciate that you are trusting me on your journey to a better you. Now, thank yourself for deciding that today is the last day you are going to let anything hold you back from the life that you want. You are worth every penny you spent, on this journal, and every word that you will place on the page. This is your life and your legacy in the making. This is you finally choosing YOU over all things and I hope that it feels damn good!

What are some of your favorite quotes?

Write anywhere on the page

"For what it's worth, Its' never too late to be whoever you want to be.   I hope you live a life you're proud of, and if you find that you're not, I hope you have the strength to start over."
– F. Scott Fitzgerald

SECTION I: INTRODUCTIONS

BRIEFLY DESCRIBE WHY YOU BOUGHT THIS JOURNAL

THE START OF YOUR JOURNEY

MENTAL HEALTH SHOULD NOT BE TABOO

POSSIBLE THERAPY OPTIONS

Briefly explain where you are currently, mentally, emotionally and what made you purchase this book.

_____

_____

_____

_____

_____

_____

_____

_____

_____

_____

_____

_____

_____

_____

_____

_____

_____

_____

_____

_____

The Start of Your Journey

THE START OF YOUR JOURNEY

Learning how to be happy, in the eye of the storm, will not take the voodoo spell that one might think it requires. It's like everything else, you have in life, it takes working for it constantly. Just like the degree you obtained, the career you have or anything else you have thrown your passions into, it will take constant effort on your part. Anything worth having is worth working for and happiness is no different. It's crazy that the hardest problems usually have the simplest solutions to them. What is even crazier, is that most of us, cannot even phantom a life without our internal struggles. Yes, those struggles have shaped us in to who we are, but we often forget that, that's not *all* we are.

As a person who has struggled with anxiety and depression my whole life, I knew, I could not stand another day on earth not trying to change that narrative. It took me going deep inside myself to gather up my painful memories, bad experiences, disappointments I couldn't get pass and start tackling them one by one.

In my journey to self-discovery, it was a hard pill to swallow to learn that all the sadness, anger, negativity and frustrations that I felt were *self-inflicted*. While most of the things I went through, weren't my fault, constantly reliving those negative experiences, almost on a daily-basis, were. It was a self-defeating thought process that ended-up becoming my default setting.

I was both a prisoner and the warden of my own mind; all the while I was holding the key to my freedom in my hand. I could not envision a life where I could be happy with all that I had been through. Especially, since the pain that I felt, was still as strong as it was the day it happened, all those years ago. I stayed bound to my pain and if I'm being completely honest, there was times that, that's all I wanted to do. My pain was as familiar to me as my own reflection. I tried the usual ways of numbing the pain, by trying to stuff it down and ignore it. I even bought it a new dress, took it out to dinner, was convinced that falling in love with someone who wasn't me, would help me forget. I tried everything I could think of, except confronting my problems head on.

Yes, exploring emotional and mental pain isn't fun. It doesn't feel good and it shouldn't. Negative experiences are horrible enough to go through the first time and revisiting those experiences, will most certainly, reopen old wounds.

The difference this time around, will be when you decide to change your whole mindset on why you are currently revisiting the past. It won't be to just feel pain or to feel sorry for yourself, but a determination that this will be the last time. The last time you are going to allow your pain to have power over you. The only objective for delving into your painful past is to get the experience behind you once and for all. By gaining power over your emotions and how you react to the old and the new, is one of your greatest assets into gaining inner peace and moving forward with your life. I'm sure we have all learned by now that life is not a bed full of roses and that you have often had to suffer in silence. Please know that you are not required to keep suffering through life. Life is meant to be lived, not endured.

In this book, I hope that you will be able to dig deep and pull out every sucky part of yourself, that no longer aligns with who you want to be or how you would like to feel. Making the conscience decision to release the mental and emotional anchors that weigh so heavily on you, is a great first step, into your healing process. Writing things down, getting them out of your mind and out of your heart, can have you feeling freer and much lighter. Think of it as moving through life with *purpose*, on *purpose*, for a *purpose*. It is never too late to become who you could have been or who you were destined to be all along. Keep reminding yourself that you are not your past or your pain. You do deserve whatever you are willing to put-in the work to go get. In the short amount of time we have on earth, you owe it to yourself, to make the rest of your life, the best of your life.

- Can you imagine a day of not having to deal with the constant negative push and pull of your mind, that could derail your entire day?

- Can you imagine how it would feel, if you were able to get to the very root of the problem that has you so closed-off and struggling within yourself?

- Can you imagine having less conflict in your life, both internally and externally?

If you can, I do believe that this journal will help get you started in the right direction and serve as an invaluable tool to have with you during your journey. Writing is one of the most useful tools you have at your disposal to rid yourself of unwanted negative thoughts and energy. It allows you to free-up so much mental and emotional space by purging it out of your system. I have also made it easy for you to get started. I have created a series of worksheets, Q & A sections, deep journal prompts to get you started on your way. If you find that you run out of writing space, don't hesitate to continue your thoughts on a separate piece of paper. Once completed, tape and place the extra notes inside your journal, next to the correct journal prompt for safe keeping.

Helpful tips

Step 1. Get it all out. Whatever negative feelings of betrayal, abandonment, resentment, anger, embarrassment and so on, get them out of your mind and onto paper. Compile a list of everything that you can't let go of and haven't healed from. That way, you can see what areas you need to tackle first. Write as many details as you can remember and do so without censoring yourself. Once you finish your list, place inside of an envelope and tape it inside your journal, for safe-keeping. Then move on to the self-discovery portion of this journal

Step 2. After you have written about your experiences, walk away from it for a few days. Then revisit what you wrote to see if anything needs to be added. Next, read what you wrote out loud. How does reading it out loud, make you feel now? Are you still experiencing the same emotions as you did, when you were writing it all down? Has the emotions lessen or gained any strength? If yes, continue to ad to you letter, until it is all out.

Step 3. For the situations that you are finding no longer affect you like they once did, you can write a final letter about the situation decide to add it to the Closure list. (The closure list located further in the book.) For the situations, that still bother you, decide how you would like to heal from the problem. In some instances, that may involve you confronting someone in person, over the phone or in writing. Or you may like to save the problem to be discussed with a licensed therapist. Whatever way that you decide to work through it, just make sure that you see it all the way through to the end. In doing so, you can finally have much needed closure. Just remember, not every situation or experience needs to be dealt with or confronted, only the ones that still causes you pain or confusion.

Mental Health Should not Be Taboo

MENTAL HEALTH SHOULD NOT BE TABOO

Did you know that the quickest way to get to happiness is to stop pretending like nothing is wrong with you? It's to stop suffering in silence, but secretly wishing to be rescued. There's seems to be this whole dynamic with people not wanting to look weak and lost, which have them trying to bury their pain in plain-sight. The problem is, the more we try to pretend like nothing is wrong, the more unbalanced we get and the more that ticking-time-bomb that keeps being suppressed will be ready to explode.

We all know that allowing that ticking bomb time to fester and go off can cost you everything. It can cost you your relationships, your friends, your job and even your freedom. Some look at it as, being strong and holding on. I say, what a complete waste of strength it is in trying to hide your vulnerability. There is strength in asking for help. It is better to put your strength to better use towards healing, rather than wasting time on trying to be strong. Whether you hide your problems or not, without notice or permission, trials and tribulations of life will keep coming. You do not have to go at it all alone. Seeking counseling or the support of a trustworthy friend, can do wonders.

Choosing Counseling

Deciding to seek counseling is a great way to help explore your past endeavors in a practical and sensible way. A therapist can help you to breakdown exactly what it is that makes you tick and help you understand how underlying emotions tend to influence your decision-making. Finding the right counselor will ensure the maximum benefits that you can receive. Although, it's not as simple as booking your first appointment. You need to vet your potential therapist. You need to be comfortable enough with your chosen counselor to be able to "open up" to them or it won't work. Consider a counselor that not only hears you, but one who is committed to helping you heal, in the specific ways that you need to be healed.

Every therapist has their own style and approach to administering therapy. It's better to ask, up front, what those practices are, so you aren't wasting time with the wrong counselor. You don't want to sit down with a counselor who expects you to take the lead (if you can't) or one who automatically takes the lead by deciding on what you will focus on first. You are allowed, to decide how your therapist and their style of therapy would benefit you.

I can't tell you how many times that I have sat down in front of the wrong counselor feeling uncomfortable or feeling like I wasn't being heard. Or worst having a therapist who only think you should focus on the positive things in your life, while glossing over the bad, in a "but-look-how-far-you've-come" stance.

If accomplishments or success in life healed emotional wounds, then the dynamics of suicide among successful people wouldn't exist. I personally needed a counselor to help me gain different perspectives on the things that I went through, while *also* reminding me that I had come a long way with my accomplishments. I didn't need a cheerleader and neither do you. You need exactly what you came for, someone to help you to heal from your past. If, at any time, you feel you are not getting what you need from your therapist, cancel your future sessions and move on. You are not obligated to stick with someone or an approach to therapy that doesn't suit you. You can choose someone else, whenever you need to. Now, I don't recommend looking for the "perfect" counselor, because there is no such thing. Your focus should be on whether you will be able to build a working relationship with your therapist.

Support circles

If you're still not convinced that seeking outside therapy is right for you, maybe you can rely on or build a support circle. Building a wellness circle is like a support group of people you already know and trust. They are not licensed therapist, who are equipped with directing you how to deal with a wide range of complex issues. Your support circle can only do so much in helping you, especially if your support circle is dealing with similar issues at the same time as you are. Yes, you can gain different perspectives and be able to bounce ideas off each other. Just talking things out can be a great resource. Also, remember that support groups will also need to be supported, as well. Be the lending ear and helpful person that you yourself desires. Your circle will need you just as much as you need them. So, it's imperative that you afford them the same kind of support.

While there is nothing wrong with relying on other people to help you get through life trials, remember that healing is an inside job. Having a support system that we can count on is great, just try not to abuse your circle. Try not to burn them out. Especially, if they are going through their own problems themselves.

- Who is in your support circle/group?
- Is this arrangement beneficial to you?
- Whose support circle are you apart of? Are you beneficial in this arrangement?

For those you of fighting depression

It might feel a little tougher to escape your past, but it is very much possible, to break the rinse, dry, repeat cycle of despair. Even while you are still standing in the eye of your own storms. You should recognize that you are, at least, still standing. Depending on what stage of depression you are in, you may need to ask for help, sooner rather than later. Remember asking for help, is not a weakness, it is displaying strength. Until you are fully ready to take that next step with counseling, take time to get it out of your head. Have someone or a hotline on speed dial that you can call, if things get to be too much. You do not have to go at this alone. Someone does and will care about what you are going through, if given the chance. In the meantime, take extra care of yourself, by utilizing some self-care techniques. There are worksheets later in the book to help you flesh out some ideas to coax you out of depression.

For those who are still on the fence

If seeking counseling or therapy is still not something you are ready for, that's okay too. Use this book as a tool to get everything out of your head and on paper. Think of this as a first step. So, when you are ready to work with someone you will know exactly where you need to start. This book will allow you to have everything all in one place. Remember, having an outside perspective on the things that are too much for you to handle could be the very thing that you need to get you on the path of healing. Lastly, before you dive-in, let's remember that to get through your pain, you need to first acknowledge that you have things you haven't healed from. Be prepared to dig-deep and being brutally honest in how you are feeling. Remember, the deeper the honesty, the bigger the healing.

Health Insurance Benefits Options

Check with your insurance company to ask about your mental health benefits. Depending on your insurance carrier and before you start paying your co-pay, you can get a certain number of sessions with no out-of-pocket expense. Most employers' benefits programs provide EAP benefits (Employee Assistance Program) that provide you with a hotline where you can call and talk to someone anonymously. You can retrieve the information regarding your benefits package on the employers' website. You can also check with your local community health centers that provide mental health services either free or on a sliding-fee-scale.

Other options

- National suicide hotline 1-800-273-8255
- The Trevor Project 1-866-488-7386
- https://suicidepreventionlifeline.org
- You can also research specific support groups, by googling "x-y-z support groups near me."
- Considering a holistic or religious approach to counseling maybe beneficial as well.
- Online therapy is now "a thing" and can sometimes be cheaper than in-person therapy.

Helpful Tips

- During your first session, feel free to interview your potential therapist, to see if there is a potential match to your needs.
- Do you like them, do you like the energy you feel from them? Do you feel like you would be heard?
- Do you like their approach to therapy?
- Do you feel heard, respected and comfortable, opening up to them with your deepest thoughts?

List of possible therapy options

_____

_____

_____

_____

_____

_____

_____

_____

_____

_____

_____

_____

_____

_____

_____

_____

_____

_____

_____

SECTION II: SELF-DISCOVERY

PROFILE

QUESTIONS TO GET THE WHEELS TURNING

SELF-DISCOVERY QUESTIONNAIRE

WHAT DO YOU NEED TO EXPLORE FURTHER?

JOURNAL PROMPTS QUESTIONS

DESCRIBE THE DEPTHS OF YOUR CLOSES RELATIONSHIPS

SUPPORT CIRCLES + WORKSHEETS

THE BEST OF YOUR + WORKSHEETS

PAINFUL TRUTHS ABOUT YOURSELF + WORKSHEETS

TOXIC BEHAVIOR + WORKSHEETS

EMOTIONAL TRIGGERS + WORKSHEETS

WHAT UPSETS YOU WORKSHEET

WHAT MAKES YOU HAPPY WORKSHEET

SELF-CARE EMOTIONAL TRIGGERS WORKSHEETS

SELF-DESTRUCTIVE EMOTIONAL TRIGGERS WORKSHEETS

WHAT DID YOU LEARN ABOUT YOURSELF

TOPICS I COULD USE OUTSIDE COUNSELING WORKSHEET

TOPICS I CAN HANDLE ON MY OWN WORKSHEET

Profile

Name	
DOB	
Career	
Married/Single	
#Kids	
Religion	
Introvert/Extrovert	
Zodiac Sign	

What else is important to list here?

_____

_____

_____

_____

_____

_____

_____

_____

_____

_____

_____

Questions to get
the wheels turning

Questions to get to the wheels turning:

How many times have you genuinely been happy in the last year?	
How many times have you been depressed in the last year?	
How often have you experienced anxiety or panic attacks in the last year?	
How often have you not felt like yourself in the last year?	
Are you feeling stuck?	
Do you feel supported by your family and friends?	
How well have you taken care of yourself mentally, emotionally and physically in the last year?	
Are you using any form of drugs or alcohol or other behaviors in self-destructive ways, to cope or get through the day emotionally and mentally?	
How often do you revisit the past?	
How many times have you felt hopeless or directionless this year?	
How open are you to accepting change?	
How open are you to confrontation and dealing with hard situations?	
Are you living the life you sought after, once upon of time?	
Have you experience a great loss in your life? Have you dealt with it?	
Do you have financial stressors, that you feel you aren't handling well?	

How much "me time" do you allow yourself?	
How often do your unfilled expectations let you down?	
Do you know how to ask for help?	
If you don't know how to ask for help, why?	
Do you tend to play small, in order, to make other people like you?	
Do you come from a dysfunctional family?	
Do you care how your family feels about who you date?	
Does being a part of your family, enlist a sense of pride in you?	
If you had a chance to start your life over, would you take it?	
Do you function better when you are around a lot of people?	
Do you need a lot of people in your life to be happy?	
Do you require a lot of money, in order, to be happy?	
Do you feel like you are able to be yourself, no matter who you are around?	
Do you wait for other people to help solve your problems?	
Are you open to seeking counseling or therapy?	
Do you feel that you are the only thing holding you back in life?	

Self-Discovery Questionnaire

The next worksheet is for you to get a feel for how well you know yourself and how you react to certain situations. The questions are random and are in no particular order. You should highlight any of the questions that you may wish to explore further.

A=Always AA=Almost Always S=Sometimes AN=Almost Never N=Never N/A=Not Applicable	
I am very reliable.	
I am trustworthy.	
I am who I say I am, and people can count on that.	
I often feel forgotten about.	
I often feel like people are always judging me.	
I am easily offended by other people words and actions.	
I have personal routines that make my life easy.	
I have personal routines that make my life harder.	
How ambitious are you? Also, scale 1 to 5? **(5 being the highest)**	
How love-oriented are you? Also, scale 1 to 5? **(5 being the highest**)	
How career-oriented are you? Also, scale 1 to 5? **(5 being the highest)**	
How family-oriented are you? Also, scale 1 to 5? **(5 being the highest)**	
I can handle confrontation, when dealing with hard situations.	
I do not make excuses for my bad behavior.	
I tend to blame others based solely on my own assumptions.	
I am aware of my own toxic behavior.	
I can handle being called out on my own bullshit.	
Do you find that you push people away?	
Do you think you know what is best for other people?	
Do you find it easier to help others pursue their dreams and passions, than to pursue yours?	
How often do you feel alone, surrounded by people?	

I feel self-conscience around other people.	
I feel loved and accepted by my family and friends.	
I feel a lack of funds is the biggest stressor in my life.	
I feel having more money would change my life.	
I often give up on my dreams and goals.	
I am often easily annoyed or impatient.	
I tend to handle rejection badly.	
I tend to avoid my problems when they seem to be too much.	
I often use sex, as a way, to deal with stress or loneliness.	
I often drink or do drugs to cope with my feelings.	
I tend to handle everything in stride.	
I love the ins and outs of my family life and routines.	
I am often told that I can be rude.	
I often feel that I am misunderstood.	
I often feel criticized and not seen as good enough.	
I tend to withdraw from people when I'm feeling insecure or inadequate.	
I am often told that I am confrontational.	
I tend to never fully forgive someone once they betray me.	
I often use food to cope mentally and emotionally.	
How often do you feel needed by the people in your life?	
I often anticipate the needs of others.	
I often put the needs of others before my own.	

I feel like my life is on a constant overload.	
I get overwhelmed when things don't go as intended.	
I tend to recklessly lash out when I'm hurt.	
I am, able to, admit to when I am wrong and apologize.	
I tend to make a lot of impulse decisions, when I am stressed out.	
In bad situations, I can own up to my part in it.	
I tend to feel hopeless or worthless at times.	
I usually surround myself with people of value.	
I am constantly searching for more out of life.	
My mother had a huge influence on my life decisions. **T/F**	
My father had a huge influence on my life decisions.	
I am aware of the toxic relationships in my life. **T/F**	
I often put-up walls to keep people from hurting me.	
I often procrastinate on handling things that need to be done.	
My mind often drifts into negativity.	
I feel there is time to turn my life around. **T/F**	
I am good a telling people what I need in my life.	
I am comfortable in my own silence.	
My past failures keep me from taking other risks.	
I often give up on things that seem too hard.	
I have things in my life to be grateful for. **T/F**	
I am a great listener and can communicate effectively.	

In an argument, rather than to respond, I listen to understand.	
I can handle being outside of my comfort zone.	
I know how to give myself enough credit for my successes.	
I feel uncomfortable talking about my problems to other people.	
I often think no one really cares about what I go through.	
It's easy for me to express my feelings.	
It's easy for me to tell people exactly how I feel.	
I can say NO to things I don't want to do.	
I still have anger that I am still holding on to from my past. **T/F**	
I still have resentments that I am holding onto from my past. **T/F**	
I am aware of the toxic family members in my life. **T/F**	
I am aware of the toxicity of my intimate relationships. **T/F**	
I have to get even with people who hurt me.	
I am aware of the people whom I have hurt.	
I know what makes me happy.	
I know how to stand-up for myself.	
I often feel stuck in my career.	
I often lean on a higher power to get me through tough times.	
I never let others sway my ideas and thought processes.	
I am not afraid of making my own mistakes.	
I often feel like my life is not going in the direction I want it to go.	
I treat myself with respect.	

I expect to be treated with respect.	
I know how to let myself go and have fun.	
I am an easy person to be around and get to know.	
I find it easy to make friends.	
I often sensor myself around people to make them comfortable.	
I can often be manipulative to people to get what I want.	
I prefer to be rescued from my problems.	
I often listen to my intuition when making decisions.	
Being around other people tends to drain my energy.	
I tend to learn things the hard way.	
I find it hard to accept another person's advice.	
I need to spend a lot of time around other people.	
I can readily identify who is in my support system.	
My fears tend to keep me from going after the things I truly want.	
I often go to bed feeling unfulfilled or unhappy about my life.	
How authentic or true to yourself are you? Rate yourself to 5. **(5 being the highest)**	

Time to Tally up

Highlight the areas you would like to explore further

A / T	AA	S	AN	N / F	N/A

What do you need to explore further?

1.
2.
3.
4.
5.
6.
7.
8.
9.
10.
11.
12.
13.
14.
15.
16.
17.
18.
19.
20.

Journal Prompt Worksheets

Describe how it was growing up with your mother/maternal figure. What lasting effect did she have on you growing up?

Describe how it was growing up with your father/paternal figure. What lasting affect did he have on you growing up?

_____

_____

_____

_____

_____

_____

_____

_____

_____

_____

_____

_____

_____

_____

_____

_____

_____

_____

_____

_____

_____

_____

Describe how it was growing up without your absentee parent. What lasting effects did it have on you growing up?

_____

_____

_____

_____

_____

_____

_____

_____

_____

_____

_____

_____

_____

_____

_____

_____

_____

_____

_____

_____

_____

If you grew up an orphan or in foster care, describe the impact it had on you growing up. Describe your feelings about your experience.

_____

_____

_____

_____

_____

_____

_____

_____

_____

_____

_____

_____

_____

_____

_____

_____

_____

_____

How best would you describe yourself and your personality? Do you often feel misunderstood? By whom?

_____

_____

_____

_____

_____

_____

_____

_____

_____

_____

_____

_____

_____

_____

_____

_____

_____

_____

_____

How do you think people perceived or judge you? What do you wish they could see in you or think about you?

_____

_____

_____

_____

_____

_____

_____

_____

_____

_____

_____

_____

_____

_____

_____

_____

_____

_____

_____

_____

_____

How were you expected to turn out as an adult? As told to you. Did you make the mark or go in another direction?

_____

_____

_____

_____

_____

_____

_____

_____

_____

_____

_____

_____

_____

_____

_____

_____

_____

_____

_____

Do you have a secret you are expected to take to the grave? Describe how it affects you to carry this burden?

_____

_____

_____

_____

_____

_____

_____

_____

_____

_____

_____

_____

_____

_____

_____

_____

_____

_____

_____

If you could sit and talk to someone who has hurt you that have passed away or left your life, what would you need to say to them?

Describe a time when you betrayed someone's trust in you. What happen and how did it affect your relationship with that person?

_____
_____
_____
_____
_____
_____
_____
_____
_____
_____
_____
_____
_____
_____
_____
_____
_____
_____
_____
_____
_____
_____

Describe a time when you went to counseling or therapy. What influenced your decision to go? Was it helpful or unhelpful?

Describe the type of family dynamics, that you believe, that you grew up with. Are you from a close-knit, toxic or distance family?

_____

_____

_____

_____

_____

_____

_____

_____

_____

_____

_____

_____

_____

_____

_____

_____

_____

_____

_____

_____

_____

Describe a time when you were truly heartbroken. No matter the relationship or situation.

If you experienced any kind of abuse, what lasting affects did it have on you?

_____

_____

_____

_____

_____

_____

_____

_____

_____

_____

_____

_____

_____

_____

_____

_____

_____

_____

Describe how it was growing up with your siblings/other family members. Or describe how it was growing up as an only child. What impact did it have on you?

_____

_____

_____

_____

_____

_____

_____

_____

_____

_____

_____

_____

_____

_____

_____

_____

_____

_____

_____

_____

_____

_____

_____

_____

Describe a time, in your life, when you felt that you were at the lowest point mentally and emotionally.

_____

_____

_____

_____

_____

_____

_____

_____

_____

_____

_____

_____

_____

_____

_____

_____

_____

_____

_____

_____

What childhood memories and/or beliefs did you grow up with that you feel shaped your life for good or bad? Describe the biggest, greatest or worst impact.

What was your greatest disappointment or defeat that shaped the way you think, act, love or make life decisions?

_____
_____
_____
_____
_____
_____
_____
_____
_____
_____
_____
_____
_____
_____
_____
_____
_____
_____
_____
_____
_____
_____
_____
_____

Describe a time when someone important to you really let you down. How did it affect you?

_____

_____

_____

_____

_____

_____

_____

_____

_____

_____

_____

_____

_____

_____

_____

_____

_____

_____

_____

Describe how you usually deal or cope with stress, when you are experiencing unhappiness.

What have you been holding on to all these years that you haven't been able to forgive yourself for and why?

Describe a time when you truly regretted hurting someone else. Is it possible to make amends?

What are your views on having faith in a better tomorrow? Do you think increasing your faith will help you through this journey?

_____

_____

_____

_____

_____

_____

_____

_____

_____

_____

_____

_____

_____

_____

_____

_____

_____

_____

_____

Describe what would make or force you to completely give up on someone previously close to you.

Describe what doesn't help you, during your healing process. What is more beneficial to you?

Describe how well you deal with people leaving your life.
Whether through breakups, death, or by other means.

Describe a time when you were ready to give up and throw in the towel, but you didn't. What made you keep going?

_____

_____

_____

_____

_____

_____

_____

_____

_____

_____

_____

_____

_____

_____

_____

_____

_____

_____

_____

_____

_____

_____

When you are in a bad place emotionally or mentally, describe your overall mood and interaction with other people.

Describe any generational curses that you believe have shaped how your family interacts with each other. How does it affect you personally?

Describe the anger or resentment that you feel, that you simply cannot let go of, regarding a person or life event.

Give a hard assessment of the people in your life. Who adds value, deducts value, is neutral, toxic or just difficult and requires patience?

What part of yourself are you afraid of showing, to other people, at the risk of feeling vulnerable or exposed?

Describe an incident when you have either felt completely used or unwanted.

What parts of your life feel more complicated than it needs to be?

How aware are you of your affect in other people lives? How do you feel you make a difference in a good or bad way?

Describe a time when you really wanted something important and did not receive it. How did it affect you?

Describe a situation or a memory that still haunts you, to this day. What is it and why?

_____

_____

_____

_____

_____

_____

_____

_____

_____

_____

_____

_____

_____

_____

_____

_____

_____

_____

_____

_____

_____

_____

What was the hardest lesson that you have had to learn? How does this lesson still affect your life now?

When faced with difficult situations or people, how do you respond or communicate?

Describe the last time that you were feeling completely depressed. Describe how you were able to come out of it?

_____

_____

_____

_____

_____

_____

_____

_____

_____

_____

_____

_____

_____

_____

_____

_____

_____

_____

_____

_____

_____

Describe the depths of your close relationships

Who are they? Length of time? Are you satisfied with this union? Does any relationship need work? List any positives or negatives.

Who:	Length of time:
Relationship to you:	Does the relationship need work?
How satisfied are you with the depth of this relationship?	

Who:	Length of time:
Relationship to you:	Does the relationship need work?
How satisfied are you with the depth of this relationship?	

Who:	Length of time:
Relationship to you:	Does the relationship need work?
How satisfied are you with the depth of this relationship?	

Describe the depths of your close relationships

Who are they? Length of time? Are you satisfied with this union? Does any relationship need work? List any positives or negatives.

Who:	Length of time:
Relationship to you:	Does the relationship need work?
How satisfied are you with the depth of this relationship?	

Who:	Length of time:
Relationship to you:	Does the relationship need work?
How satisfied are you with the depth of this relationship?	

Who:	Length of time:
Relationship to you:	Does the relationship need work?
How satisfied are you with the depth of this relationship?	

Support Circles

Who is in your Support Circle?

Who are they? What do they provide? Best form of contact? Are you apart of their support circle?

Who:	Length of time:
Form of contact:	Are you apart of their S/C?
How do they support you?	

Who:	Length of time:
Form of contact:	Are you apart of their S/C?
How do they support you?	

Contact list:

_____

_____

_____

_____

_____

Who is in your Support Circle?

Who are they? What do they provide? Best form of contact? Are you apart of their support circle?

Who:	Length of time:
Form of contact:	Are you apart of their S/C?
How do they support you?	

Who:	Length of time:
Form of contact:	Are you apart of their S/C?
How do they support you?	

Contact List:

_____

_____

_____

_____

_____

Support Circle Worksheet

Who are they? What do you provide? Best form of contact?

Who:	Length of time:
Form of contact:	Are they in your S/C?
How do you support them?	

Who:	Length of time:
Form of contact:	Are they in your S/C?
How do you support them?	

Who:	Length of time:
Form of contact:	Are they in your S/C?
How do you support them?	

Support Circle Worksheet

Who do you support? What do you provide? Best form of contact?

Who:	Length of time:
Form of contact:	Are they in your S/C?
How do you support them?	

Who:	Length of time:
Form of contact:	Are they in your S/C?
How do you support them?	

Who:	Length of time:
Form of contact:	Are they in your S/C?
How do you support them?	

The Best of you

The Best of you

(Describe your best traits from your perspective)

Personality Traits	Physical Traits
1.	1.
2.	2.
3.	3.
4.	4.
5.	5.
6.	6.
7.	7.
8.	8.
9.	9.
10.	10.

Communication Traits	Character Traits
1.	1.
2.	2.
3.	3.
4.	4.
5.	5.
6.	6.
7.	7.
8.	8.
9.	9.
10.	10.

The Best of You

(Your best traits described by your trusted circle)

Personality Traits	Physical Traits
1.	1.
2.	2.
3.	3.
4.	4.
5.	5.
6.	6.
7.	7.
8.	8.
9.	9.
10.	10.

Communication Traits	Character Traits
1.	1.
2.	2.
3.	3.
4.	4.
5.	5.
6.	6.
7.	7.
8.	8.
9.	9.
10.	10.

Painful Truths About Yourself

PAINFUL TRUTHS ABOUT YOURSELF

Hate to break it to you, but you are not as perfect or innocent as you may want to believe you are. We are all human and we humans make a lot of mistakes and yes that includes you! We all have personality traits that aren't as loveable or likeable as you would hope. We do things and say things that get on other people nerves. We have habits that simply rub people the wrong way.

It may be hard to hear or accept this, but it won't stop it from being true. We are not perfect beings and thank God we aren't! Could you imagine being the only person on earth with that kind of burden? One slip up and having everyone finding out about it, has got to be a recipe for disaster. Who needs that? Not me and hopefully not you either. The only thing we should worry about is putting the best version of ourselves forward and being better than we were yesterday.

In the next exercise, write down the things you know that aren't the greatest about your personality. Not so you can be hard on yourself, just honest. Next, seek out people who you can trust to give it to you straight. The people who will give you an honest assessment about you and your personality traits, without trying to destroy you in the process. Remember, you should only seek out people who you trust and know that you have a real friendship with. Again, the point of this exercise is to get to know yourself completely. Find out things about your personality that you may need to work on or keep the same. The answers may surprise you, some may even shock you, but these are things you need to know. When I went through this experience, I was shocked to find out things about myself in both a negative and a positive light. So, don't be afraid to hear the good, the bad or the ugly. You are a work in progress, like everyone else is and you are in the process of becoming the best version of yourself. So, use this information to your advantage.

Helpful tips

Remember when asking someone (or multiple people) their honest opinion of you, respect their honesty and don't use their answers against them or your relationship. If the relationship is real for both parties, then you should be able to handle hearing anything they have to say. If it's bad, then look at it this way, "Hey, this person knows what kind of mess I can really be, and they can see the value of having me in their lives."

Things that are a bit unsavory about your behavior and traits, you should take the necessary steps to correct the behavior. Especially, if you are just learning, how your ways are affecting someone else and is probably putting a relationship you value in jeopardy. Lastly, save the attitude or defensive rebuttals, they are only giving you the helpful information that you need and asked for. They should feel free to do so without retribution.

Painful Truths About Yourself
(from your perspective)

Personality Traits	Insecurities
1.	1.
2.	2.
3.	3.
4.	4.
5.	5.
6.	6.
7.	7.
8.	8.
9.	9.
10.	10.

Communication Traits	Character Traits
1.	1.
2.	2.
3.	3.
4.	4.
5.	5.
6.	6.
7.	7.
8.	8.
9.	9.
10.	10.

Painful Truths About Yourself

(by your trusted circle)

Personality Traits	Insecurities
1.	1.
2.	2.
3.	3.
4.	4.
5.	5.
6.	6.
7.	7.
8.	8.
9.	9.
10.	10.

Communication Traits	Character Traits
1.	1.
2.	2.
3.	3.
4.	4.
5.	5.
6.	6.
7.	7.
8.	8.
9.	9.
10.	10.

Toxic Behavior

TOXIC BEHAVIOR

Again, you are not always the victim you think you are. Things are not only and always happening to you, despite what you think. The painful truth is, sometimes you suck too! I mean that in the nicest possible way! ☺

We are all guilty of doing or saying things that we shouldn't. We all have put things out into the atmosphere that we wish we could take back. We all have those little funky and quirky things about our personalities, that are just off-putting to others. We all can be annoying, needy, rude, uptight, sleep deprived, physically and emotionally exhausted, time challenged and a host of other things no matter what it is, we aren't always at a 100% every day. That's all a part of being human and alive.

Those behaviors become an issue when a person is completely unaware of their toxicity toward other people. If you are aware of your toxic behavior and you decide that unless challenged, you don't need to change your ways, you are dead wrong. If you find yourself always replacing people, in your life, or hanging-out with a new circle every so often, then the problem with your relationships is probably you. Do you find that you tend to push people away, but are hurt when they leave? People will exit stage left, out of your life, simply because you pushed them away and it won't be their fault either. So, if you push, make sure you want them gone.

Toxic behavior is just another form of self-destructive behavior, there is always a root cause for the way that you are acting and sabotaging your relationships in the process. When dealing with all your emotional and mental baggage, you need to find healthier ways to deal with the issues that are truly bothering you and those things are usually deep-rooted. A licensed professional is a great place to start, when needing to get to the core of these problems. How aware are you of your own toxic behavior?

Are you likely to be the person?
- Who must get the last word?
- Who threaten or enact violence?
- Who twist the truth or bring up old arguments, in new situations?

- Who like to bring up old childhood or past topics to suit their current agenda?
- Who likes to bring up old childhood or past topics of trauma, as an excuse for current behavior?

Do you tend to:
- Take everything personally?
- Obsess about negative thoughts?
- Treat yourself like a victim?
- Lack empathy for others?
- Need constant validation?

Are you prone to:
- Lying?
- Being unapologetic?
- Not willing to admit your mistakes?
- Blaming others for your actions or words?
- Any form of abuse, physical, emotional or mental?
- Talking poorly about others?
- A constant need to be in control of everything and everyone?
- Manipulative when the situation is going isn't your favor?
- Refusing to listen to other people concerns or feelings?
- To starting drama and then turning into the victim?

Helpful tips

- Remember you don't have to be a horrible person, to have toxic ways.
- Don't push people away and expect them not to leave.
- Don't belittle or be passive-aggressive because things aren't going your way, just to get a response and/or reassurance. You just might get the opposite of what you are looking for.

A list of MY Toxic Behaviors

Behaviors I recognize or were told to me by my peers

1. _____
2. _____
3. _____
4. _____
5. _____
6. _____
7. _____
8. _____
9. _____
10. _____
11. _____
12. _____
13. _____
14. _____
15. _____
16. _____
17. _____
18. _____
19. _____
20. _____

Emotional Triggers

EMOTIONAL TRIGGERS

Do you know what your emotional triggers are and how they affect you? When you are feeling sad, what normally works to pull you out of that sadness? Maybe one of the ways you like to coax yourself out of sadness is for you to drink an entire bottle of wine, with a side of a whole pizza, while you watch Netflix and chill solo. That is something that you could add to your self-care habits, if it makes you feel better. On the flipside, maybe eating a whole pizza and drinking an entire of bottle of wine is something that you would put on your self-destruct list. That is something that only you can decide. Remember, the only person that gets to read this is you. So, there is no judgement here. Just be honest with yourself and the ways that you cope. Decide, at the end of the exercises, if there are changes that need to be made in how you handle yourself emotionally.

You should be able to practice self-care techniques, when you are emotionally triggered. So, that you can avoid falling down the rabbit hole of despair, especially if you are prone to depressive episodes. Having written reminders may also be helpful; when you are really feeling depressed and need something to remind you that you *can* get through it.

In my journey, to self-discovery, I notice that the shape my current environment, directly affected how clear my thinking was at the time. In order to get my thoughts together, I first had to clean up. Only then was I able to figure out a solution to whatever problem that was originally stressing me out.

Do you know what most of your triggers are?

- Are you prone to self-defeating or destructive behaviors, surrounding a certain emotion?

- Do you know of any specific self-care techniques that can potentially turn everything around?

- I designed two sets of worksheets that list a few common emotional triggers to be filled out with the normal ways that you usually handle yourself, when emotional problems arise.

A list of My Emotional Triggers

That I Recognized and what was told to me.

1. _____

2. _____

3. _____

4. _____

5. _____

6. _____

7. _____

8. _____

9. _____

10. _____

11. _____

12. _____

13. _____

14. _____

15. _____

16. _____

17. _____

18. _____

19. _____

20. _____

Sound off and release anything that upsets you

Write anywhere on the page

Things that upset
me...

Record anything that makes you happy

Write anywhere on the page

Self-Care

SELF-CARE

You can't run yourself into the ground, by trying to be everything to everyone and for every cause. Everyone needs to know how to implement ways that helps them whine down and relax. On the self-care worksheet, write down the way you would normally handle yourself with care next to the emotional trigger given. If you don't have a certain way that you provide yourself with self-care, you can write down things that you might like to explore and see if it can be a technique that can be beneficial in the future.

Next, research all the areas of your life and see if anything on your to-do-list can be eliminated or at the least scaled-back. Search your day to day routines, job responsibilities, time-consuming tasks, religious obligations and so on and so forth. Eliminate what you can so that you can pencil in some much needed "me time". To focus on you and you alone, so you can recharge your batteries. Even a small window of time can do wonders. How much free time do you see for yourself in the future?

Mon	Tues	Wed	Thru	Fri	Sat	Sun

Self-Care Emotional Triggers

SAD	
PETTY	
PISSED OFF	

FORGOTTEN	
ANGRY	
LONELY	

TAKEN FOR GRANTED	
LIED TO/ON	
FEELING PLAYED	

MENTALLY DRAINED	
MISUNDERSTOOD	
EMOTIONALLY OUT OF SYNC	

Self-Care Ideas

(That I have researched and is open to trying)

1. _____
2. _____
3. _____
4. _____
5. _____
6. _____
7. _____
8. _____
9. _____
10. _____
11. _____
12. _____
13. _____
14. _____
15. _____
16. _____
17. _____
18. _____
19. _____
20. _____

Self-Destructive Behaviors

SELF-DESTRUCTIVE BEHAVIORS

We all have things that can trigger us to spiral out-of-control or divulge in self-destructive behaviors. Write-on the adjoining worksheets how you usually respond to the written emotional trigger. Do you respond by consuming excessive amounts of food, starvation sex, religion, isolation, physical mutilation spending, gambling, alcohol or drugs? Do you know these are just the tip of the iceberg of self-destructive habits? However, you normally respond decide if there is another way to handle what you are feeling; rather than giving into your emotion. Do you know if your self-destructive ways are hurting more than just you? Has anyone brought anything to your attention? Even if your habits seem harmless or under control to you, you may be causing others unnecessary stress.

Questions to ask yourself

- When things are stressful and draining, to cope, what are your self-destructive behaviors that you use?

- Are you aware of how any of your self-destructive behaviors are affecting more than just you?

- Are you using food, drugs, alcohol or sex in excessive amounts just to cope? Are you spending excess money you don't have, on things you don't need?

- Are you aware of the root cause of why you use such methods (in excess) to cope? Is it time to talk to a professional or seek treatment?

A list of my 'bad habits'

(That I acknowledge or was told to me)

1. _____
2. _____
3. _____
4. _____
5. _____
6. _____
7. _____
8. _____
9. _____
10. _____
11. _____
12. _____
13. _____
14. _____

Self-Destructive Emotional Triggers

SAD	
PETTY	
PISSED OFF	

FORGOTTEN	
ANGRY	
LONELY	

TAKEN FOR GRANTED	
LIED TO/ON	
FEELING PLAYED	

MENTALLY DRAINED	
MISUNDERSTOOD	
EMOTIONALLY OUT OF SYNC	

What did you learn about yourself?

Is there anything that surprised you about yourself? List the things that you are proud of or comfortable with learning about yourself as well as things that you need to explore further.

1. _____

2. _____

3. _____

4. _____

5. _____

6. _____

7. _____

8. _____

9. _____

10. _____

11. _____

12. _____

13. _____

14. _____

15. _____

16. _____

17. _____

18. _____

19. _____

20. _____

Possible list of topics that I could use outside counseling

List the topics here:

2. _____

3. _____

4. _____

5. _____

6. _____

7. _____

8. _____

9. _____

10. _____

11. _____

12. _____

13. _____

14. _____

15. _____

16. _____

17. _____

18. _____

19. _____

20. _____

List of topics that I can handle on my own

List the topics that you can handle on your own, without any help?

1. _____
2. _____
3. _____
4. _____
5. _____
6. _____
7. _____
8. _____
9. _____
10. _____
11. _____
12. _____
13. _____
14. _____
15. _____
16. _____
17. _____
18. _____
19. _____
20. _____

SECTION III: MOVING FORWARD

LETTING IT ALL GO

In an effort of emotionally and mentally purging ourselves into a much more peaceful state of being, there will be times where we will have to just let certain things *go*. If nothing can be done to change the situation, decide if it is still worth holding on to. Try giving up the ghost and release the power it had over you. You will thank yourself later.

Not everything you have been through needs to be fixed, reconciled or dealt with. Sometimes changing your feelings about a specific situation or person, will be all you need, in order, to move forward. Release yourself and move on.

If, a true amends cannot be reached (by two willing parties) do not allow yourself to keep holding on to anything that can't be changed. There is no need to grovel or beg to get in someone "good graces" when you are met with unreasonable resistance, especially after a sincere effort was made to make things right.

Who hurt you?

Who has hurt you? Are you willing to forgive and let go?

1. _____

2. _____

3. _____

4. _____

5. _____

6. _____

7. _____

8. _____

9. _____

10. _____

11. _____

12. _____

13. _____

14. _____

15. _____

16. _____

17. _____

18. _____

19. _____

20. _____

FORGIVENESS

There will come a time in your journey, when you are going to have to learn to forgive and let go of certain things. Learning to forgive someone even without an apology, will give you back your power over the situation.

Practicing the art of letting go is a surefire way to stop letting a person or a situation keep you clinging to the past. No longer will it have power over your thoughts, your actions and your emotions. Your power will belong to you and you alone. You will start to care very little about all the apologies you haven't and probably will never receive.

Stop letting the absence of an apology hold you back, from pushing forward and moving on. If you never get that heartfelt apology that you feel you deserve, you will still have to find a way to let it all go. Forgiveness is as much for you as it is for the other person, if not more for you. You should be too busy dealing with the facts and deciding if someone or a situation needs to be addressed at all. Sometimes, no apology is the best apology you can receive. You don't know what seeing the other person who hurt you can trigger in you; causing you to start the process of healing all over again.

Some situations like abuse of any kind, no amount of apologizing to you, will ever correct the wrong it caused. Yet, you will still need to figure out a way to heal yourself from constantly reliving the event. To ensure that you can put the situation behind you for good, you will have to find a way to heal from the experience itself.

Helpful tips

- Remember forgiveness is more for you than it is for them.

- Don't hold back on your growth or potential to move forward, by waiting for someone to give you permission to heal. Learn to heal with or without them. Their lack of an apology shouldn't be contingent on whether you get to move on or not.

- Don't blame yourself or rationalize your abuse. You were not in the wrong place at the wrong time. They were! You are not to blame for someone's horrible actions against you.

- If you are not strong enough to let a situation go on your own, please seek professional help.

Who have you hurt?

Who have you hurt and are you planning to make amends?

1. _____

2. _____

3. _____

4. _____

5. _____

6. _____

7. _____

8. _____

9. _____

10. _____

11. _____

12. _____

13. _____

14. _____

15. _____

16. _____

17. _____

18. _____

19. _____

20. _____

ATONEMENT

We seem to always be "in our feelings" about something, either past or present. No matter how hard you try to mask your pain, those intense emotions are always seeking to be released and the ugly truth is "hurt people," almost always hurt other people. You have, most likely, hurt and did things to other people knowingly and unknowingly. We often tend to release that hurt onto the wrong people. Instead of hurting or confronting the person who hurt you, we tend to take-it-out on the ones closest to us.

Should you consider making atonement for your wrong doings, remember this, holding on to guilt and shame, can cut just as deep as holding on to pain caused by someone else. Those very same emotions of guilt and shame can have you holding yourself back from happiness, as well. It can remind you of all the things you have done wrong and make you feel unworthy to receive the forgiveness, you need to move on.

Think back to a time, when you cause someone else pain, does it still haunt you? Do you think it still haunts them? No matter how justified you feel you were in your actions, do you often think that maybe, just maybe, you might of went just a horse whisper too far? Then there is that little thing called Karma. Karma doesn't care what the situation was or who was at fault, but she will be there taking notes and you can bet your last, that she will be visiting you later. Consider making atonement if something is still on your heart or mind. Making a sincere amends, could be the very thing that can free you.

Helpful hints

- Admitting when you are wrong, is not only maturity, but a good way to show love and respect.

- It's okay to be a good person, who do bad things, but it's not okay to stay that way.

- Don't let your pride harden you, just accept the responsibility of your actions and do what you can to correct it.

- If you value the relationships you currently have, and a riff is created, you should feel obligated to do what is necessary to fix your part. Remember you are only half of the equation; no relationship can be fixed if all parties involved aren't open to it. Accept what it is and move on from the situation.

- Saying I'm sorry to someone you value, shouldn't be hard. Never let your pride be the reason that one of your best relationship goes sour.

- Try putting yourself in their shoes and see how you would have responded to your words and actions. How would it go over for you?

Atonement List

Who do you have to make amends too and Why?

1. _____

2. _____

3. _____

4. _____

5. _____

6. _____

7. _____

8. _____

9. _____

10. _____

11. _____

12. _____

13. _____

14. _____

15. _____

16. _____

17. _____

18. _____

19. _____

20. _____

CLOSURE

We all have a short time on this earth, and we don't know the day or the hour, when our time is up. Do you want to waste it on being bitter, angry or depressed? We weren't put on earth to just suffer and learn lessons. We were put here to experience all that life has to offer. Believe it or not that includes some great stuff, if you're open to it.

As we know, a painful past has a sneaky way of making our present and future decisions for us, based on unsettled emotions that can seriously set you back. Gaining control over your thoughts and emotions can have you focused on all the right things and can help you keep all other things in perspective. That's why learning to put the past behind you and gaining closure is so necessary, so you can stop setting your future self, up for failure.

Decide to keep the door of the past closed and tack an "out of business for good" sign on the door, so all the madness can end there. It's never too late to get things back on track and to start living in the *now*.

Closure List

What do you need to have closure on? How do you plan go about it? Self-help, confrontation or counseling?

1. _____

2. _____

3. _____

4. _____

5. _____

6. _____

7. _____

8. _____

9. _____

10. _____

11. _____

12. _____

13. _____

14. _____

15. _____

16. _____

17. _____

18. _____

19 _____

20. _____

Counseling Worksheet

List the topics that you need to seek outside therapy, so that the issue is behind you.

1. _____

2. _____

3. _____

4. _____

5. _____

6. _____

7. _____

8. _____

9. _____

10. _____

11. _____

12. _____

13. _____

14. _____

15. _____

16. _____

17. _____

18. _____

19. _____

20. _____

Self-help Worksheet

List the things that you can tackle on your own, without needing outside help.

1. _____

2. _____

3. _____

4. _____

5. _____

6. _____

7. _____

8. _____

9. _____

10. _____

11. _____

12. _____

13. _____

14. _____

15. _____

16. _____

17. _____

18. _____

19. _____

20. _____

MID-POINT CHECK-IN

How are you feeling so far? I know things have been quite emotionally and mentally exhausting for you, but it's going to be so worth it in the end. Remember the goal is to release the past and plan out ways to make the rest of your life the best of your life. You should keep going to get to the best part. Never stop and wallow in the pain, without getting to the best that is yet to come.

You now have reached the point in this journal where you can now decide how you want to turn your life around and start charting a new course. You can have the life you want and the one that you truly deserve, if you are willing to work for it. Use the next set of journal entries to freely express how you are feeling at this point in your journey. Then get ready to move on to my favorite part of this journal...moving forward!

How am I feeling so far?
(Mid-point check-in)

_____

_____

_____

_____

_____

_____

_____

_____

_____

_____

_____

_____

_____

_____

_____

_____

_____

_____

_____

_____

_____

SECTION IV: FINDING PURPOSE AND VISION

FINDING PURPOSE AND VISION

What is purpose and how do you find it? My understanding of purpose is a person being able to be happy while doing something with their life that makes them feel like they matter; while also making some sort of contribution to the world. It doesn't mean you have to live some extravagant life, nor does it need approval of others, for you to feel great about it.

Your purpose can literally be anything. You will know when you are in your purpose, because it will not only feel good but, you will start to feel like a void has been filled. If your purpose and passions can also make you money, well that's just the icing on the cake.

I have personally struggled for years to figure out what my purpose was and what provided me with the most joy. I knew always wanted to write a book, but I let my fears of not being good enough, get in the way. I often wondered who in their right minds would listen to me or care what I had to say. I totally talked myself out my dreams constantly, too worried that I would fail. If I had of just moved out of my own way a long time ago, I could have possibly written a book or became a published author much sooner. Writing for me, whether its fiction or non-fiction, provides me with so much joy, I can't believe I denied myself this much happiness, for so long. Every word I put on a page, (even if I thought it was crap, at some point) makes me feel like, this is all I ever wanted to do. I just had to give myself permission to do it, whether I good or bad. Besides anything you practice long enough, you will eventually get better at it, right?

When you start to think about what your purpose could potentially be, keep in mind a few things.

- Figure out what it is you are good it or what sparks joy.
- Decide if sharing your talents with other people, would be beneficial to them or not.
- Does this talent you hold, necessarily, translate into you having a serious passion for it?
- Decided if you never pursued this option, could you forget about it? It is said that the one thing you can't stop thinking about doing is your purpose calling you. Do you agree with that assessment?

What I hope you don't consider purpose to be, is something that is supposed to make you filthy rich. It's certainly okay if it does, however, know that it's okay if your purpose or calling in life doesn't revolve around making money. I mean, who doesn't want to live a comfortable life, with all the bells and whistles, just make sure your happiness isn't dependent on you having said bells and whistles.

Looking into your life, what do you see for yourself in the next five years? Are you fine with the way life is going for right now or do you have a different vision? Who and what is included in this vision? Are you married with kids? Are you happily single and jet setting all over the world? Can you even find the time to take the necessary steps to get into your purpose? Use the table below to see how much time you could potentially have to work on new goals, with any free time you have during your week.

According to your personal routines, where could you free-up time to pursue goals?

Mon	Tues	Wed	Thru	Fri	Sat	Sun

What are you talented or skilled at?

_____

_____

_____

_____

_____

_____

If you could change the world, one problem at a time, what would it be?

_____

_____

_____

_____

_____

What does success look or feel like to you?

_____

_____

_____

_____

_____

What would you like to be known for, in the present and future?

_____

_____

_____

_____

_____

What does it mean to have a purpose?

_____

_____

_____

_____

_____

Who do you admire and believe that they are living in their purpose?

_____

_____

_____

_____

_____

_____

T= True F= False S = Sometimes N/A = Not Applicable	
Finding my purpose, in life, is very important to me.	
I feel lost without a clear purpose of what I'm doing in life.	
I know what living in your purpose looks like.	
I believe not knowing your purpose in life causes depression.	
I feel like people judge me for my lack of success.	
I judge another person success by what they have or what they do.	
I need luxuries to know that I am living a successful life.	
I believe success and purpose is intertwined.	
I believe one's purpose is to be in service to others.	
I feel like time is running out for me, in finding my purpose.	
If I never go after my dreams, I will regret it forever.	
I do not care how other people judge the way I live.	
I do not equate luxuries or way of life as being successful.	
There are too many obstacles in going after my dreams.	
I envision my dream-life as being modest, but comfortable.	
Every time I fail at something, it makes it harder for me to start something new.	
I believe my degree helped steer me towards my purpose.	
If I could start my life over, I would.	
I firmly believe that failure is an integral part of success.	
It hurts when my support system fails to understand my dreams.	
I'm used to having no support, when it comes to following my dreams.	

What do you wish you would have known about life 5, 10, 15-20+ years ago?

_____

_____

_____

_____

_____

_____

_____

_____

_____

_____

_____

_____

_____

_____

_____

_____

_____

_____

_____

_____

_____

_____

Describe your proudest accomplishment, so far?

What do you think is too late for you to achieve, in your life? Why?

_____

_____

_____

_____

_____

_____

_____

_____

_____

_____

_____

_____

_____

_____

_____

_____

_____

_____

_____

_____

What dreams or goals have you, repeatedly, put on the back burner?

Describe the life skills that you feel you weren't taught before entering adulthood. Have you learned those skills along the way?

Describe the biggest fear you have about your life. What would you do, if it came true?

Rate what you think of your life so far. Have things been easy, fair or hard? What lessons have you learned along the way?

Describe what your biggest regrets could be, if you never get around to making them a reality.

LAW OF ATTRACTION

The Law of Attraction is something that I just recently stumble upon in the last few years or so. I can honestly say I have witness positive changes in my life, just from having a more positive mindset. The Law of Attraction or LOA is the ability to attract into our lives whatever we are focusing on. In basic terms, all thoughts turn into things eventually. Attraction which uses the power of the mind to translate whatever is in our thoughts and materialize them into reality. The premise of if you focus on negative doom and gloom you will remain under that cloud. If you focus on positive thoughts and have goals that you aim to achieve you will find a way to achieve them with massive action.

While I whole heartily love the premise surrounding LOA, I also firmly believe that faith without work is dead. You can have a positive thought process all day long about achieving your goals, but unless you put action behind those thoughts, you are probably going to be doing the eternal wait. Even if applying LOA in your life, only produces small victories, aren't those better than a bunch of negative things happening? Once you have it in your mind that you want something, you should pray about it and believe that what you have asked for will in fact happen. It's called having faith and believing that you deserve what it is you are asking for.

Lastly, when considering using the Law of Attraction to try and manifest things into your life, remember that the main ingredient is positive thinking. Positive thinking can do more for you than having a negative mindset ever will. The next time you come up against an unpleasant experience or situation, try responding to it in a positive way. Instead of immediately getting upset, ask yourself, "is this worth ruining my mood over?" When you don't allow your emotions to take over a situation, you lessen the chances of your emotions taking control of the situation. You lessen the chances of something small becoming bigger than it really needs to be. It's not always easy to try and control your emotions but try to make an honest effort going forward. It could make all the difference, in the way the rest of the day will end up falling into place.

Helpful tips

- Ask yourself, if getting upset is worth ruining your entire day?
- Will this situation matter in a week or a few months from now?
- Am I willing to allow someone to pull me into their crappy day?

VISION BOARDS/MOOD BOARDS

Vision boards and mood boards are simply visual reminders of the things you say you want, and you must work at to get. These are your goals. These are things that you give a specific deadline to complete, usually within a year. The things you put on your vision board should be near and dear to your heart's desire. It should also correlate with the overall vision you have for your life or the way you envision your life going.

Remember, the images and pretty fonts and clever quotes aren't going to leap off the board and manifest themselves into your life, you will have to put in the necessary work to make it happen. Are you ready to transition into the person that is needed in order step into your destiny?

If you want to be a world class traveler, are you going to be able to put aside the necessary funds to be able to book the trip? If you want to meet the love of your life, are going to make yourself available to the outside world or continue to stay in the house waiting for a miracle? *Faith without works is dead. †* So, roll up those sleeves, decide on a plan and get to it!

Write anywhere on the page

Write small descriptions or words.

Current Life Evaluation

Your life As Is...Up until now. List the priorities that are important, that you are proud of or dissatisfied with.

LIFE

CAREER

LOVE

Dream Life Possibilities

What does your dream life entail, if there were no restrictions of any kind, in the terms of money, time and resources? The sky's the limit.

L
I
F
E

C
A
R
E
E
R

L
O
V
E

The change I want to see in myself or my life

Write anywhere on the page

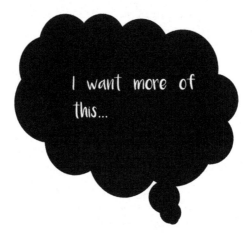

I want more of
this...

The change I want to see in myself or my life

Write anywhere on the page

I want less of this...

The things I DO have CONTROL over

Write anywhere on the page

The things I have <u>DO NOT</u> CONTROL over

Write anywhere on the page

Things that
are NOT in my
control...

Current Goals

6-month Goal	Barriers	Plan of Action

1-year Goal	Barriers	Plan of Action

Updates:

Future Goals

6-month Goal	Barriers	Plan of Action

1-year Goal	Barriers	Plan of Action

Updates:

Family Goals

6-month Goal	Barriers	Plan of Action

1-year Goal	Barriers	Plan of Action

Updates:

Fitness Goals

6-month Goal	Barriers	Plan of Action

1-year Goal	Barriers	Plan of Action

Updates:

Other Goals

6-month Goal	Barriers	Plan of Action

1-year Goal	Barriers	Plan of Action

Updates:

My Bragging Rights

List all the goals and accomplishments that you have already completed.

1. _____

2. _____

3. _____

4. _____

5. _____

6. _____

7. _____

8. _____

9. _____

10. _____

11. _____

12. _____

13. _____

14. _____

15. _____

Goals and Accomplishments, I'm in the process of...

List all the goals and accomplishments that you are in the process of making.

1. _____

2. _____

3. _____

4. _____

5. _____

6. _____

7. _____

8. _____

9. _____

10. _____

11. _____

12. _____

13. _____

14. _____

15. _____

FEAR LIST

Before your fears about the present and the future get the best of you and try to derail your plans; release them out of your mental space and get them down on paper. That way you can stop processing unnecessary data in the background that causes you to procrastinate. Release your thoughts and emotions, so that you can get back to planning and working on your dreams.

Instead of thinking...	Try considering...
What if I'm not good enough?	What if you are more than enough?
What if it doesn't work out?	What if it does work out?
What if I fail?	What if you don't?

Fear List

What scares you about your future? Where do you think that you could possibly fail in your career, love-life, family, and future goals? You can also add insecurities and trust issues here too.

1. _____

2. _____

3. _____

4. _____

5. _____

6. _____

7. _____

8. _____

9. _____

10. _____

11. _____

12. _____

13. _____

14. _____

15. _____

16. _____

17. _____

18. _____

19. _____

20. _____

How am I feeling, after this Journey?

Write anywhere on the page

I am proud of
myself for...

GRATITUDE

Life isn't about having things seem perfect, in order, to be happy. You don't need to have your complete heart's desire, in order, for you to feel thankful. Taking time to feel gratitude for all the things you have, the health you feel, the way your basic needs are being met, is more than a reason to feel gratitude. You must learn to steal away little moments in this crazy life. No matter what you are facing, you will be able to recognize all things you *don't* have to face. Nothing in life is perfect.

- Your finances aren't great, but you still have an income.
- You don't live in a 5-star mansion, but your house is either paid off or your mortgage can be managed on one income.
- You don't have the ideal partner, but you feel loved by them when it counts.

Small moments of gratitude are fleeting. However, if you try to focus on enough of the small moments they tend to multiply. If you sit still for a moment. I bet you can count at least 10 very important things that you can totally feel grateful for. So, instead of focusing on the things you don't have try focusing on the things that you do. Luxuries don't necessarily equate to happiness. The best things in life often don't come with a price tag. What are some of the things you are currently grateful for?

Gratitude List

What am I thankful for? The big and the small things.

1.
2.
3.
4.
5.
6.
7.
8.
9.
10.
11.
12.
13.
14.
15.
16.
17.
18.
19.
20.

BONUS SECTION V: LOVE GOALS

LOVE GOALS

What is on your wish list? Your list of non-negotiables, the things you will not tolerate in a relationship. What do you bring to the table? It is important to think seriously on all the things you really need and want in a mate. These things based as close to reality as possible. Your wish list shouldn't be a "be all-end all" list. Leave some wiggle room for the person you end up meeting. Don't let fantasy trump reality, when it comes to deciding who you will invest your time in.

It's okay to be flexible in the beginning, especially since you are not likely to get a person's whole story right in the beginning. Try not to throw a fish back in the water too quickly, if they seem to still be a work in progress, especially if you're destined to be integral to their achievement. You will never know, if you never give someone a real chance. You never know what role you are supposed to play in someone's life or vice versa, upon meeting them. The point is, don't lose out a good person because they haven't trusted you enough to show you who they really are. On the flip-side, make sure that when they do show you exactly who they are, that you believe them! Try being open minded and flexible on what your mate MUST bring to the table. No one is perfect, which shouldn't automatically disqualify them, some people are in the middle of starting over.

It is a good thing to emulate the very things you desire in a mate. If you want someone that is trustworthy, you need to be trustworthy as well. You should be looking for someone that aligns with the long-term vision you see for your life. While there is nothing wrong with looking for someone that could help spice things up or add color, just remember, initial excitement usually wears off fast. Also, it is important to either maintain your previous life or go out and get one. No one person can be everything to you; they're only a missing piece of the puzzle, not the whole thing.

If you are married, how is that relationship going? Are either of you happy or is there work to be done? While the purpose of the section seems to be dedicated to the singletons, I do believe a married person can gain some insight through the up and coming exercises. As someone who have never been married, I will not pretend to know what the best advice is on keeping a marriage together. You can probably tell, at any moment soon, I'm going to suggest counseling...marriage counseling that is. I have known married couples who have sought out counseling and have come out through to the other-side, but it was also because both parties were open to the idea. I pray that, if this is the next step in your journey that you will have a willing partner. Someone who is just as committed to making your relationship work.

Good luck and try to keep an open mind, during the counseling process. Remember you need to be heard, so does your partner.

Whew! There, I did it. Hopefully, my two small suggestions on married life will not cause you to throw the book down in exasperation. Some of the worksheets can you help you discover ways to rekindle things in your marriage. Maybe you could start re-dating your partner-in-crime all over again. Just figured out ways to shake things up a little bit.

T=True F= False S = Sometimes N/A = Not Applicable	
I have been told that I have a certain type.	
I know what my type is.	
I often fantasy about the perfect love or relationship.	
I feel free to date whomever I please.	
I have already experienced my worst relationship.	
I have already experienced my best relationship.	
I require a lot attention from my partner.	
I try to give my partner the whole world if, I can.	
I am single, until I am married.	
I am easy to get to know on a personal level.	
I expect my partner to tear down the walls, I have had to build up.	
I take time to heal after every break up.	
I can forgive infidelity, when there aren't outside kids produced.	
I can forgive infidelity, even if there are outside kids produced.	
I expect my partner to guess what it is I'm feeling.	
I can handle criticism from my partner well.	
I know how to give constructive criticism to my partner.	
I hate when my partner doesn't want to spend time with me.	
I understand the whole concept of work husbands and wives.	
I see no problem with dating married people.	
I despise the ideal of dating a married person.	

I am prone to using sex as an escape or some form of healing.	
I often participate risky sexual Behavior.	
I can be emotionally or sexually manipulative.	
Being in relationships tend to bring out a lot my insecurities.	
Loyalty is very important to me in a relationship.	
I feel like I can love someone enough for both of us in a relationship.	
I need to be spoiled, wined and dined to know that I'm appreciated.	
My loyalty and respect in a relationship, is *not* free!	
I am open to being in an open and sexually fluid relationship.	
I am completely certain of my sexual health and status.	
Communication is very important to me in a relationship.	
My friends and family are often very present in my relationships.	
My friends and family approval of my partner, is very important me.	
I do not like being given ultimatums in a relationship.	
I have no problem giving ultimatums in a relationship.	
I tend to be blasé about dating a new relationship prospect.	
I tend to fall in love very quickly in the beginning.	
I tend the fall in love more slowly in the beginning.	
My partners religious practices need to mirror my own.	
After infidelity in a relationship, I tend to lose interest in my mate.	
Dating in this modern day, I feel it is way too hard.	
I usually shut down after being hurt in a relationship.	

I am often self-conscience about my weight and appearance	
I am often self-conscience about my status and social skills	
I tend to get lost or wrapped up in my relationships	
I have been told I act like a mother or authority figure in my relationships	
I think sexual intimacy is very important in a relationship	
I believe that sexual is expected, but not necessarily important to me.	
I believe in soul-mates or The One.	
I require a lot of reassurance within my relationships.	
The number of sexual partners a potential mate has had, could make me lose interest in them	
I am very forgiving within a relationship.	
I expect to be forgiven in a relationship, no matter what I do.	
I believe that relationships are doomed, once someone cheats.	
I know how to recognize someone else's love language.	
I know how to express what my love language is to my partner.	
I feel being introverted makes it harder for me to date freely.	
I tend to date bad boys or bad girls for the excitement it brings to my life.	
I understand how scandalous affairs tend to happen.	
I know exactly when someone has fallen out of love with me.	
I know exactly when someone has fallen in love with me.	
There must be a mutual sexual attraction when dating someone.	
If I am not at my best, I expect my partner to pick up the slack.	
Sometimes I can't even fantasy about being in a great relationship.	

Love Goals: Journal Prompts

Describe a time when a partner hurt you to your core.

Describe some of the normal insecurities you experience,
when in a relationship.

Do your religious beliefs play a large role in your dating routine? Is it helping or hindering your dating process?

Single and kid-free. Describe what it would feel like to you, if things stayed that way.

_____

_____

_____

_____

_____

_____

_____

_____

_____

_____

_____

_____

_____

_____

_____

_____

_____

_____

_____

_____

_____

_____

What makes you feel worthy of having your best relationship?

Describe your less than desirable traits, in a relationship, as told to you by a partner. Is there any truth to it?

Have you ever cheated while in a serious relationship? If the cheating was exposed, what did your actions cost you?

_____

_____

_____

_____

_____

_____

_____

_____

_____

_____

_____

_____

_____

_____

_____

_____

_____

_____

_____

_____

If you were cheated on, how did you handle that level of betrayal?

_____

_____

_____

_____

_____

_____

_____

_____

_____

_____

_____

_____

_____

_____

_____

_____

_____

_____

_____

Describe a relationship you were in where it made you question your self-worth. How did you handle being in that situation?

_____

_____

_____

_____

_____

_____

_____

_____

_____

_____

_____

_____

_____

_____

_____

_____

_____

_____

Describe why it hurts, if an ex moves on to a new relationship. Whether it was before you moved on or rather quickly.

Describe a time when you completely gave up on love.
What were the circumstances? Have you reconsidered?

Has sexual intimacy ever caused you anxiety or stress, within a relationship? Describe why and what you did in response to it.

How do you know when you are REALLY in love with your partner? How do you know when you are not in love?

How fast is too fast for you, when you first start dating? How do you respond when things move too fast?

How important is financial security in your relationships? Describe how your feelings would change, if money was an issue.

Have you ever had to endure any form of mental, physical, emotional or sexual abuse in a relationship? Describe.

Describe a relationship that you didn't want to end. Did it end up being a blessing or a lesson?

Describe a time you took a partner and/or relationship for granted. Describe why and who you were as a person at that time?

Describe your worst dating/relationship experience.

LOVE GOALS WORKSHEETS

Top 5 Best Relationships

1. _____
2. _____
3.. _____
4. _____
5. _____

Top 5 Worst Relationships

1. _____
2. _____
3.. _____
4. _____
5. _____

Top 5 Dates or Worst Dates

1. _____
2. _____
3.. _____
4. _____
5. _____

What do you bring to the table?

What do you bring to the table, besides your career, your lifestyle? List things about your character, personality traits, how and what a person dating you can expect being in a relationship with you.

Personality	Characteristics	Standards
Physically	Emotionally	Spiritually
Fun Stuff	In Difficult Time	Etc.

What do __THEY__ need to bring to the table?

What do they need to bring to the table, not just a career, their lifestyle? This person needs to fit into your idea vision and purpose for your life.

Personality	Characteristics	Standards
Physically	Emotionally	Spiritually
Fun Stuff	In Difficult Time	Etc.

Wish list of Qualities you want in a Mate and Relationship

These are your non-negotiables, that you will stand firm on and not alter to allow someone to fit in your life. Remember to consider your purpose and your vision for your life, when thinking about a mate.

1. _____
2. _____
3. _____
4. _____
5. _____
6. _____
7. _____
8. _____
9. _____
10. _____
11. _____
12. _____
13. _____
14. _____
15. _____
16. _____
17. _____
18. _____
19. _____
20. _____

What I never want to experience again

Write anywhere on the page

Past BAD dating reminders...

Deal breakers and Red Flags and Your No-Thank you list

These are your non-negotiables. Remember your purpose and your vision for your life.

1. _____

2. _____

3. _____

4. _____

5. _____

6. _____

7. _____

8. _____

9. _____

10. _____

11. _____

12. _____

13. _____

14. _____

15. _____

16. _____

17. _____

18. _____

19. _____

20. _____

Active Dating Ideas

List the things you've tried that did and didn't work.

What have I tried that works?

1. _____

2. _____

3.. _____

4. _____

5. _____

What have you tried that doesn't work?

1. _____

2. _____

3. _____

4. _____

5. _____

What are some potential places and ways to meet people?

1.	6.
2.	7.
3.	8.
4.	9.
5.	10.

What did you learn about yourself?

What is your love language? What are you not willing to settle for. What is on your wish list that you never knew, etc.?

1.

2.

3.

4.

5.

6.

7.

8.

9.

10.

11.

12.

13.

14.

15.

16.

17.

18.

19.

20.

Journey Reached: Congratulations!

You have reached the end of this journey. What are somethings that you want to remember about your experience?

1. _____

2. _____

3. _____

4. _____

5. _____

6. _____

7. _____

8. _____

9. _____

10. _____

11. _____

12. _____

13. _____

14. _____

15. _____

16. _____

17. _____

18. _____

19. _____

20. _____

Things to Remember, going forward

- Remember it's okay to not be O.K.! Stop suffering in silence.
- Time to take the mask off. It's time to stop braving through tough days and pretending that all is fine, when frankly, it's not.
- Not every situation needs to be fixed. Not every relationship needs to be saved. Not every incident will need an apology, in order to move on.
- Everyone processes things differently and will have different perspectives, just like two sides of the same coin.
- If it disturbs your peace, distance yourself.
- It hurts losing people or having a situation not turn out like you had hoped but holding on or playing small will ruin you.
- Choose to heal on purpose.
- You deserve to be around the people and things that create and spark joy.
- You also have the right to decide when to let go and back away from the things that disrupts your peace or healing.
- Remember how other people feel is only one piece of the puzzle. Your feelings and perspective matter too.
- If no resolution can be reached choose the next best thing, you! The best is yet to come...

Also, Coming by the Author:

The Teen Journal

The Vision Board Journal: Lifestyle Edition

Am I Ready? A Guideline to Dating with a Purpose

About the Author:

M. S. Rice is an Upstate, NY native who currently lives a nomadic lifestyle. She has a degree in journalism and is a 16-year veteran in the medical office/administration sector. She currently works as a remote medical coding specialist. Writing-journaling and all things creative have been her passions, since childhood. This is her first published book.

For more healing, wellness, self-care help, please visit the following:

The Healing Journal blog

Thehjournal.com website and online store (coming soon)

To reach the author: healingjournalproject@gmail.com

To reach the editor/proofreader: Fiverr account Patriciaarice

Also, can be reached at: healingjournalproject@gmail.com

10535633R00164

Made in the USA
Monee, IL
30 August 2019